media watch

advertising

Brenda Mann

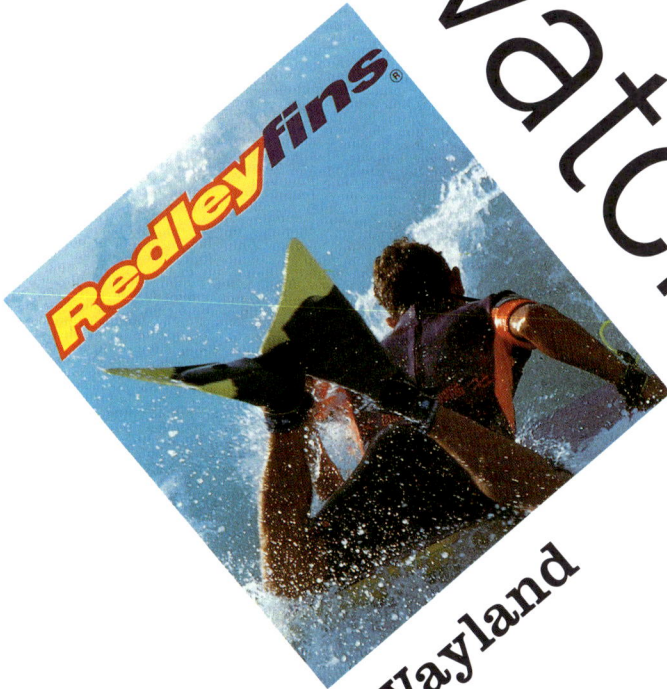

Wayland

media watch

Advertising
Newspapers
Magazines
TV and Video

Series Editor: James Kerr
Designer: John Christopher

Consultant: Julian Bowker,
Education Officer, British Film Institute.

Front cover picture: Advert for Redley swim
 fins, Australian bodyboard magazine.

First published in 1993 by
Wayland (Publishers) Ltd
61 Western Road, Hove
East Sussex, BN3 1JD

British Library Cataloguing in Publication Data
Mann, Brenda
 Advertising. - (Media Watch Series)
 I. Title II. Series
 302.23

ISBN 0-7502-0758-2

Typeset by Strong Silent Type
Printed and bound in Spain by Graficas Estella.

Picture acknowledgements
The publisher would like to thank the following for providing the pictures used in this book:
Aardman Animations/Arthur Sheriff Public Relations 28; Advertising Archives/Paul Seheult 6
(left and middle), 11,13,18,26,27,29,36,41 (bottom), 43; Barclays Bank PLC 30; John Christopher
9,21,22,24, (top); Format 5 (Brenda Prince), 41 (top) (Ulrike Preuss); Impact 19 (Mark Cator),24
(Homer Sykes), 35 (Mike McQueen); Imperial War Museum 16; Mark Power 33; Paul Seheult
6,7,8 (right), 32,34,39,40,42; Graham Smith Associates 20,22 (bottom), 23; Topham 14;
Wayland Picture Library 6 (right),15,17.

contents

what is
advertising?

The Consumers' Association, which represents buyers, claims that a young person may be bombarded by as many as two hundred advertisements in a single day. This can include eighteen commercial jingles on radio, fifty sponsored ads during a televised motor race, forty adverts at a live football match and fifty during the breaks in an evening's television. And that's not counting street posters and ads in magazines and computer games.

The Advertising Association defines advertising in this way:

> *Advertisements are messages, paid for by those who send them, intended to inform or influence people who receive them.*

This definition makes several points about advertisements. Firstly, they contain a message – that is, they have an idea they want to put over. This message may be expressed in words – 'Persil washes whiter' – or in pictures, music or jingles.

Secondly, they are paid for directly by advertisers. This distinguishes advertising from other forms of publicity, such as the use of press releases or photo-opportunities. In 1991, over £8,000 million was spent on advertising.

Thirdly, advertisements will have a purpose – to inform or influence the people they are aimed at: the target audience. For example, if you had lost your cat, you might pay to display a card in a local shop window, giving a description of the cat and a phone number to ring. Your target audience would be the local community – those who live near enough to the shops to have possibly seen the cat wandering in the neighbourhood. You are also trying to influence these people to keep an eye open for your cat and to return it to you if they find it. You may offer a reward to encourage people to respond to your advertisement. This will make your advert more likely to achieve its purpose.

RIGHT
Advertisements for shops, bars and cinemas light up a city street in Hong Kong.

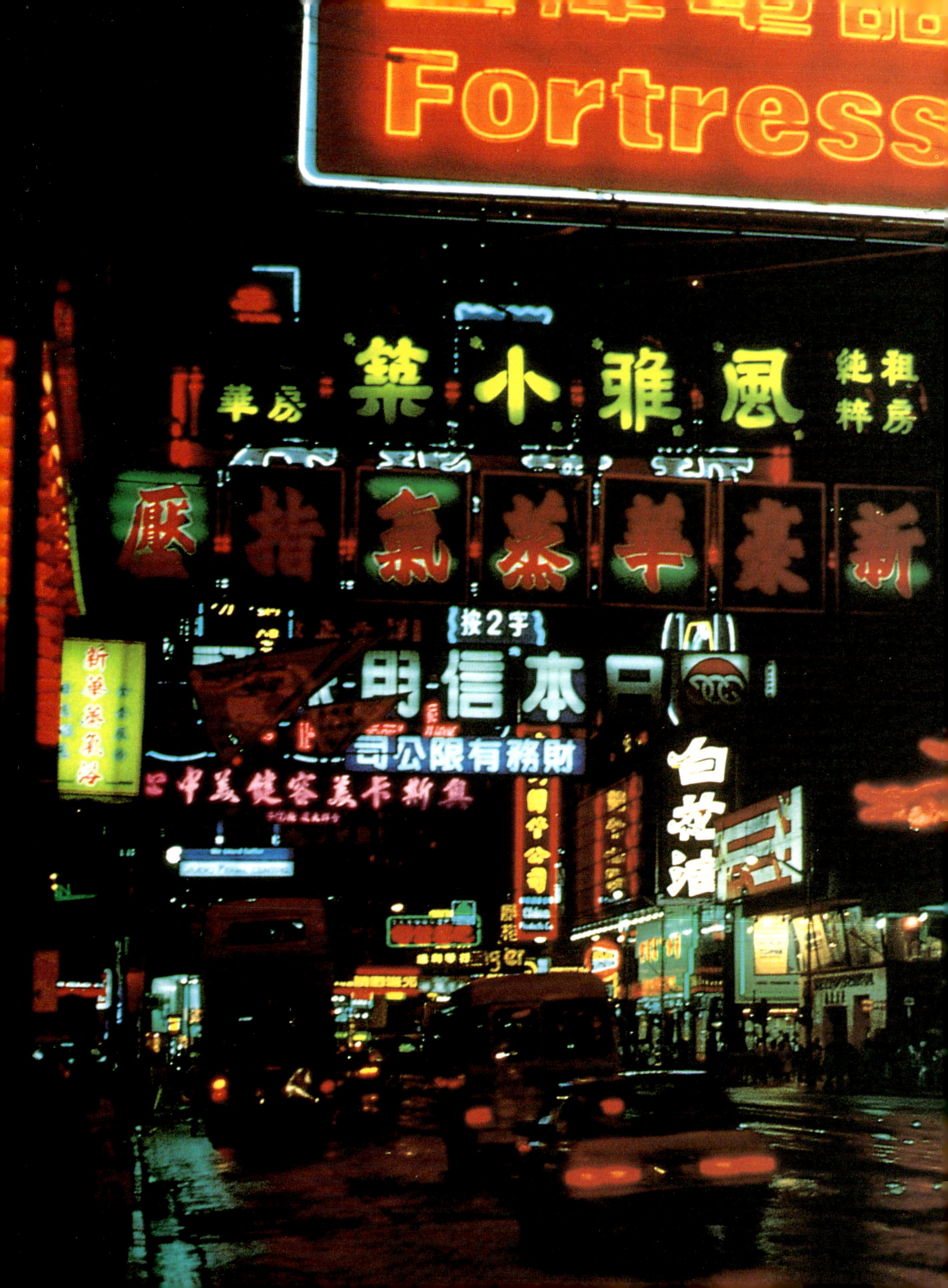
Fortress
按2字
白花油

The makers of Coca-Cola have always advertised widely. This 1926 ad associates the drink with winter sports.

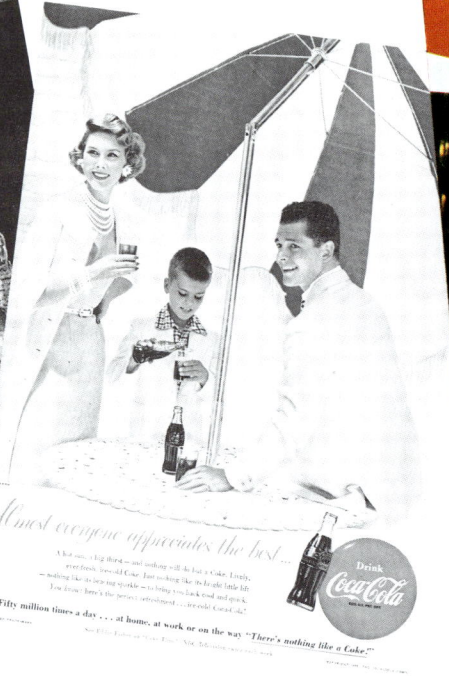

This American magazine advert for Coke from 1955 is linked to a TV advertising programme.

A recent Coke ad. The message is still the same – young, healthy people enjoy a refreshing drink of Coke.

Many ads are more obviously trying to influence us. We are all familiar with nation-wide advertisements which try to persuade us to buy a particular brand of soft drinks or ice-cream. Others try to influence groups like drug addicts or smokers to change their habits. Advertisers use a variety of techniques to attract attention and make us notice the message that they want to put across. Whatever their purpose, they will try to persuade in a way which is thought likely to work with the people they are aiming at.

The Advertisers

Many groups use advertising. The most familiar are businesses that want to sell their goods. In developed societies, advertising is an essential part of marketing products such as Coca-Cola or Nike trainers. Businesses need to let us know what they have on offer and to persuade us to buy it. New products are often launched with a national advertising campaign. Even well-established lines like Mars Bars need a high advertising profile to keep them in the public eye and fight off the competition.

The government carries out a great deal of advertising. Some government ads are merely to inform – perhaps to tell people about changes in Social Security benefits, or their rights regarding their children's school. Others are more clearly aimed to persuade, like the ads promoting the use of condoms for safer sex, or emphasizing the dangers of drinking and driving. Some government advertisements are meant to change national attitudes. A series of anti-smoking adverts in 1990 challenged the view of smoking as grown-up and exciting. They tried to make young people see it as grubby and unattractive to the opposite sex.

Governments are not the only advertisers who try to change the way people see things. Pressure groups such as Greenpeace and Friends of the Earth try to change our attitudes to the environ-ment through their advertisements. Charities like Oxfam and the National Society for the Prevention of Cruelty to Children advertise regularly to arouse sympathy for those in need and to ask for money to help them.

All these groups advertise on a large scale, spending huge sums in order to do so. But many of us are involved in advertising ourselves in a more modest way. Many schools, hospitals and youth groups advertise their car boot sales or summer fêtes in the local newspaper. People who have a bike or a computer to sell will put a classified ad in a free paper or advertising magazine. For a small payment we can put an advert in the corner shop offering our services as a baby-sitter or window-cleaner.

BELOW Government-sponsored health agencies use advertising to educate young men about the dangers of Aids.

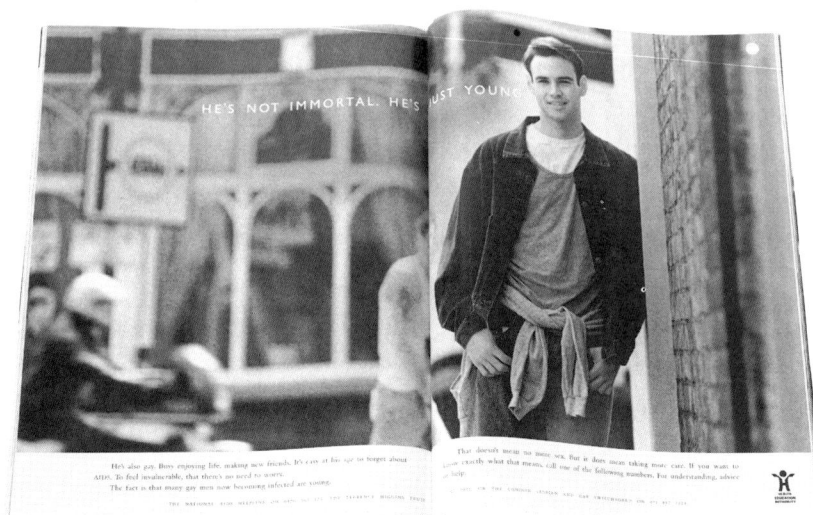

HE'S NOT IMMORTAL. HE'S JUST YOUNG

WHAT A BEAUTY.

The Media

It is important that adverts are put out at the right time and in the right place in order to reach the right people. Advertisers can choose from a variety of media according to the message they are trying to put across and the audience they are trying to reach.

More than half the money spent on advertising in the UK, (57 per cent), goes on the press – newspapers, magazines and trade directories. This includes classified advertising (small ads arranged in sections) as well as the bigger display advertisements. The advantage of the press as a medium is that adverts can be read and re-read. Magazines like *Radio Times* and other TV

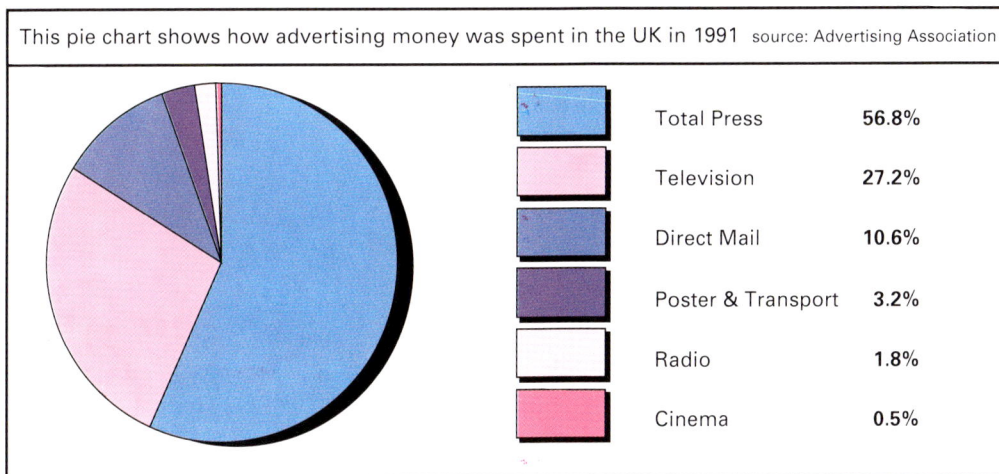

magazines stay around the house for the whole week, being picked up time and time again. Advertisers can easily target particular groups. For example, fashion houses will advertise in up-market women's magazines like *Vogue*, and software firms will target the readers of computer magazines.

The next most important advertising medium is television, with 27 per cent of advertising money. Television adverts have the impact of moving pictures which appeal to a wide audience. Voices, music and jingles can liven up the message. People watching at home are relaxed and likely to enjoy entertaining ads. The advertiser will repeat the ad, sometimes several times in an evening, to punch home the message. Audiences can be targeted through careful

This pie chart shows how advertising money was spent in the UK in 1991   source: Advertising Association

Total Press	**56.8%**
Television	**27.2%**
Direct Mail	**10.6%**
Poster & Transport	**3.2%**
Radio	**1.8%**
Cinema	**0.5%**

timing – products such as Nintendo can be plugged heavily in the late afternoon while most children are in front of the television. However, TV is an expensive medium and only the bigger companies advertise regularly.

Direct mail is advertising material that is sent direct to people's homes. In recent years, more and more has dropped on to our doormats. Often thought of as 'junk mail', it now accounts for 11 per cent of the money spent on advertising in the UK. Many people find this form of advertising irritating and intrusive, but advertisers find it a useful way of reaching a selected number of people.

'Outdoor' advertisements – posters on hoardings, bus shelters and buses themselves – are part of the urban scene. They only account for 3 per cent of advertising costs, but they are particularly effective as they are there all the time and work all day. The message must be clear and brief as the reader is likely to be on the move. Slogans like 'Guinness is good for you' became part of the language through street advertising, and posters are an art-form in their own right.

Radio advertising is popular and relatively cheap, carrying under 2 per cent of advertising costs. It is particularly good at reaching young people, many of whom listen regularly to commercial channels. Local radio stations can target local audiences. Cinema advertising (0.5 per cent) also reaches a young audience. It is perhaps the most powerful form of advertising, because cinema-goers have nothing to distract them from the messages on the big screen.

RIGHT
The simple design of this Volkswagen advertisement helps the message to stick in the memory.

Audiences

In the modern world, we have to live with advertising. We are part of the audience it is aimed at. We may enjoy it, or be irritated by it, learn from it or resent it. We may consider it art or an eyesore. The important thing is to understand how the advertising world works, so that we can make sense of it and make it work for us.

Activities

• Choose five or six advertisements from a variety of media. Explain the target audience for each and why that particular medium is used to reach that audience.

• Find two press advertisements produced by a charity or government agency. Explain how each is trying to inform and influence people.

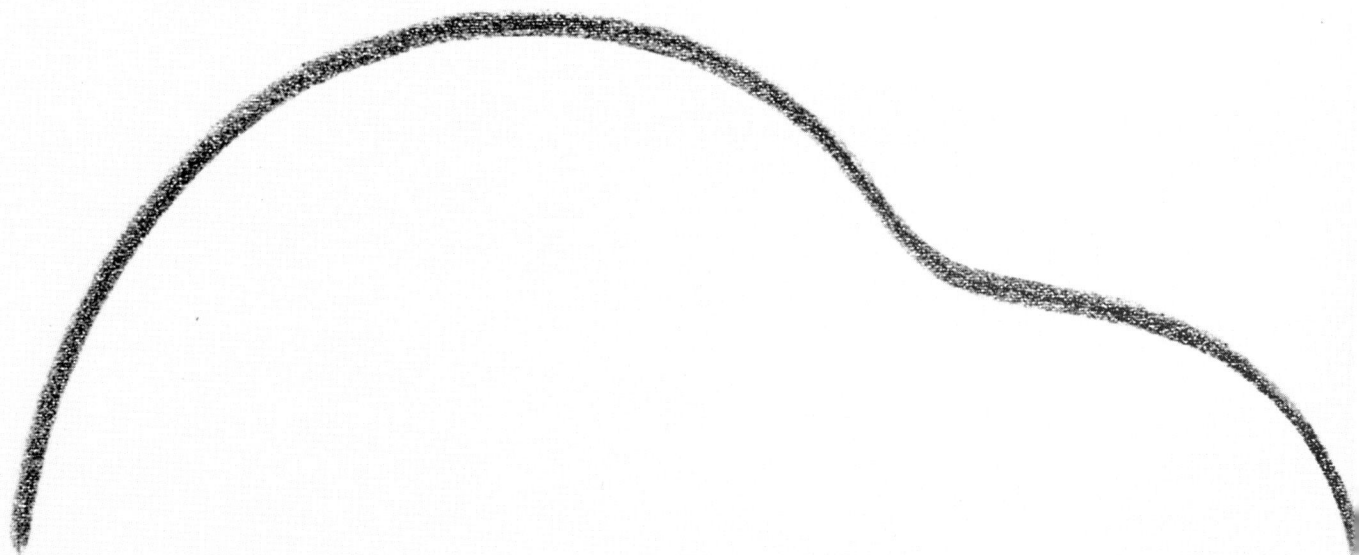

© VOLKSWAGEN OF AMERICA, INC.

The shape of things to come.

Prediction
The Volkswagen Beetle will be around for years to come.
Prediction
Someone else somewhere will introduce a new economy car and there will be lots of excitement.
Prediction
The excitement will die down.

Prediction
As in the past, people who own old Volkswagens will trade them in for new Volkswagens because (we guess) they like Volkswagens.
Prediction
Our engineers will continue to improve the way the car works and our stylists will continue to be frustrated.

Prediction
Sometime in 1972, the Beetle will become the most popular single model automobile ever made in the world, by-passing the Model T Ford with production of over 15 million vehicles.
Prediction
We won't let that last prediction go to our heads.

persuasion
past and present

Advertising is not new. In ancient times, wall-paintings advertised gladiator fights and other spectacles. In the Middle Ages, markets were noisy places with traders shouting their wares to attract passers-by. Many shops used signs and symbols to attract customers. One of the earliest was the Ivy Bush, hung above inns and wine shops. Others, which still exist today, were the three gold balls of the pawnbroker and the red-and-white striped barber's pole.

With the invention of printing, notices and broadsheets (single sheet pamphlets) began to circulate. Many were simply to give information. For example, broadsheets giving the fares and landing-places of Thames river-boats were posted in the nave of old St. Paul's Cathedral. The *Publick Adviser* was founded in 1657. This was a weekly advertising paper, which gave information on a variety of business matters. Ships waiting for cargoes were advertised, as well as job vacancies and times and fares of coaches. Books and other items for sale were listed and there were offers to trace runaway servants and apprentices.

Some adverts, as well as giving information, made extravagant efforts to persuade. In the eighteenth century, this kind of overblown advertising was called 'puffery'. Those who wrote it were 'puffers' or 'bubble-mongers'. Some early newspapers refused to accept such suspect advertisements, but most newspaper owners realized that advertisements would boost their profits. Soon, columns of advertisements were part of every newspaper, and there were few checks on their accuracy. Newspapers were often distributed through Coffee Houses, where men could meet to read, discuss news and do business. Adverts for 'Popular Pills' and 'Golden Elixirs' for all manner of ills hung on the walls along with notices of sales and shipping.

RIGHT
Victorian advertisements for pills, potions and plasters often made extravagant claims.

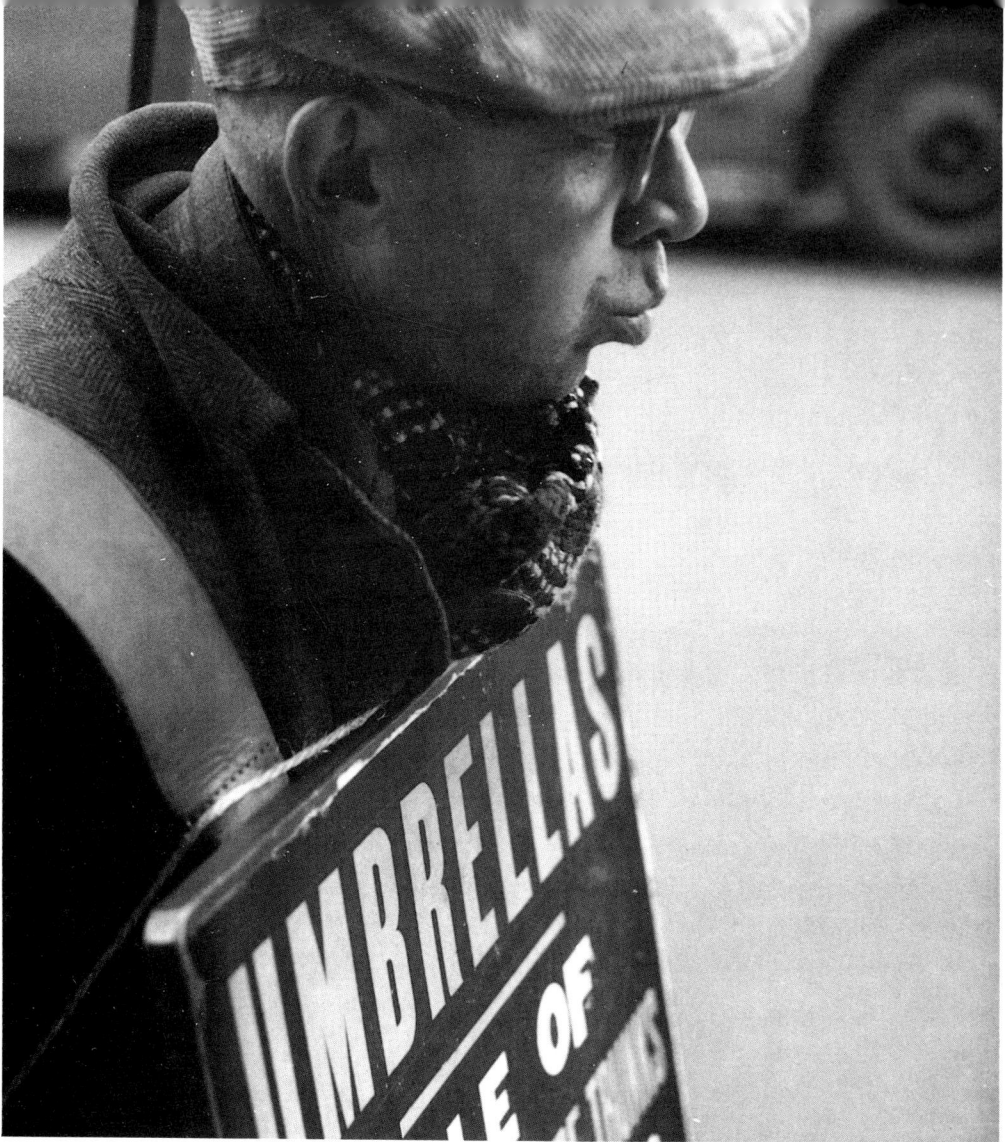

ABOVE
**A sandwich man, wrapped up against the cold,
tramps the street carrying his advertisements.**

One of the earliest illustrated adverts appeared in 1703 in the *Daily Courant.* It included a picture of an ingenious invention for making chocolate.

The nineteenth century saw the growth of poster advertising. Hoardings had to be licensed, but bill-stickers sometimes put up their posters illegally early in the morning or at night, often covering up other adverts. Sandwich men walked the streets, carrying boards advertising shops, exhibitions and other entertainments. By the 1870s, posters were often of high quality. Millais' picture, *Bubbles*, advertising Pears Soap, became one of the most famous posters of all time. In France, Toulouse-

Lautrec painted colourful posters advertising Paris night-life. This tradition has continued. Many examples of fine poster art have appeared, for example, on railways and the London Underground.

Several factors led to an explosion in newspaper advertising in the second half of the nineteenth century. The tax on press advertising was abolished in 1853. At the same time, a rapid growth in the number of businesses meant that each had to work harder to promote and sell goods. After 1870, compulsory education meant that more people could read and they demanded more lively newspapers and magazines. The popular press emerged at the end of the century, with catchy headlines, news pictures and a snappier style of writing.

As the newspapers changed in appearance, so did the adverts. They were quite different from the long, dull columns of print in the old-style press. Now they had amusing pictures and punchy headlines to press the point home. Companies became household names through slogans such as 'Beecham's Pills – worth a guinea a box!' Advertisers of Bovril and Bisto used wit and humour to attract atten-tion. New techniques were used to cre-ate new demands, desires and social habits – for example, bicycles were popularized by associating them in adverts with health, fresh air and fun. Advertisers played on the needs and anxieties of their audience in their attempts to sell body-building equip-ment, and creams to cure 'Disfiguring blotches, humiliating eruptions, and itching skin...'. These techniques are still familiar today.

The first women's page, in the *Daily Mail* (1896), enabled advertisers to target a female audience. *The Lady*, first published in 1885, and other women's magazines, provided more opportunities for reaching women. Trade and special inter-est magazines like *The Hair-dresser's Chronicle* (1866) and *Autocar* (1895) enabled advertisers to tap these spe-cialized markets.

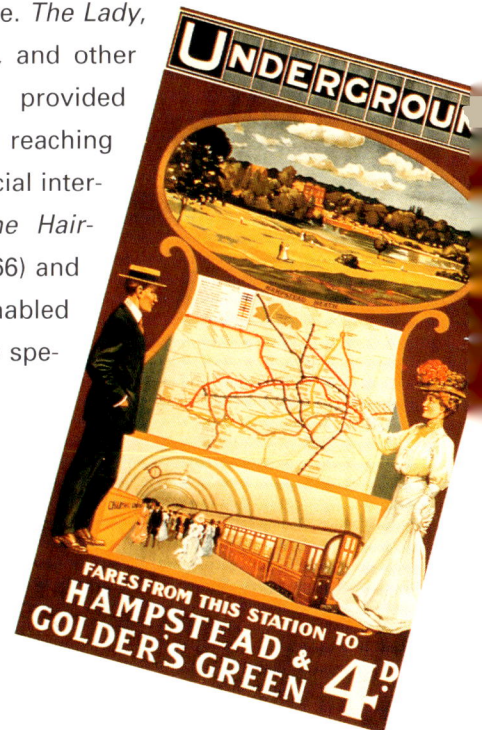

RIGHT
A London Transport poster advertises a day out on Hampstead Heath.

TOGETHER

The First World War (1914-18) saw the use of advertising to encourage young men to join the armed forces. Among the most famous was the compelling image of Lord Kitchener saying 'Your country needs you!' Advertising techniques were used for propaganda, and the lessons learned there led to the more sophisticated techniques of the 1920s and 1930s. At the same time, the advertising profession tried to crack down on untrue and exaggerated claims in adverts. In 1926 the Advertising Association was founded, which aimed 'to promote public confidence in advertising' by getting rid of shady practices. This was the age of advertising stunts. A typical *Daily Mail* promotion campaign used aircraft to write slogans in smoke trails in the sky.

In the Second World War (1939-45), the government again seized the opportunity to influence behaviour through advertising, especially in the cinema. Short, snappy and entertaining films encouraged people to 'Make do and mend' and 'Dig for Victory'. People were reminded that 'Careless talk costs lives' and the message was repeated in newspapers and magazines to increase its effect. Radio was used to cheer people up in the dark days of the war but the BBC Charter (1927) banned its use as an advertising medium.

After the war, as people became better off, the scale of advertising grew. Following the hard times of the war years, there was a flood of advertisements for consumer goods like washing machines and fridges, and such luxuries as fashion clothes and holidays abroad. As the 'affluent society' grew in the 1960s, advertisers used the increased understanding of psychology to find out what made people want to buy things. They used this knowledge to play on the unconscious hopes and desires of the audience. Vance Packard, in his book, *The Hidden Persuaders*, suggested that advertisers can influence us in ways that we are not always aware of.

LEFT
A Second World War poster emphasizes the need for the Allied nations to pull together to win the war.

BELOW
This 1950s film advertisement combines lively words and images to tempt people into the cinema.

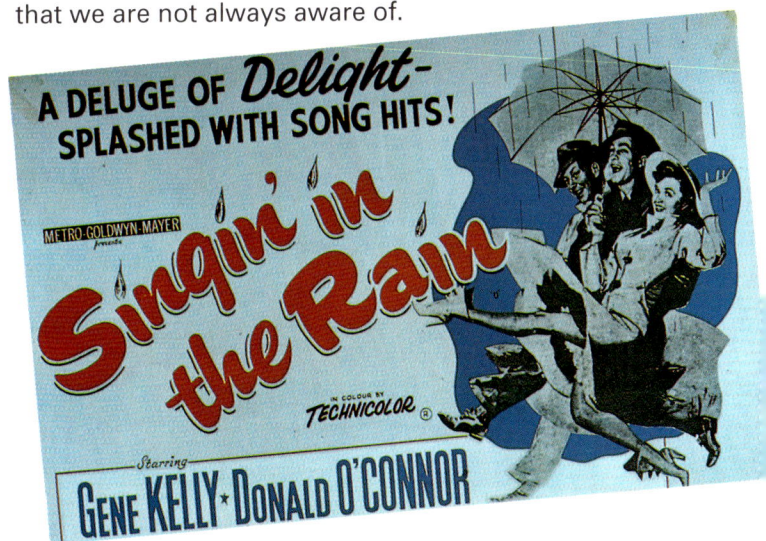

A DELUGE OF *Delight* - SPLASHED WITH SONG HITS!

METRO-GOLDWYN-MAYER presents

Singin' in the Rain

IN COLOUR BY TECHNICOLOR ®

Starring GENE KELLY · DONALD O'CONNOR

THE BONNEVILLE SPORTS COUPE FOR 1961

The well-ordered Pontiac for '61
trims width outside the wheels for better balance

Balance is the big factor in pleasant, comfortable travel!

It's achieved by distributing as much weight as possible directly between the wheels.
Pontiac '61 has more of its weight between the wheels than any other car.
You have the feeling of sitting erect even when swinging around curves and corners.

If you travel a lot . . . or just want to enjoy your travel a lot more . . . try new Wide-Track
at any of our fine Pontiac dealers. PONTIAC MOTOR DIVISION • GENERAL MOTORS CORPORATION

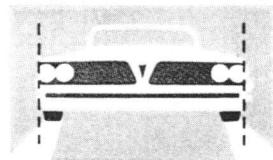

THE ONLY WIDE-TRACK CAR

PONTIAC '61—It's all Pontiac! on a new Wide-Track!

In the USA, Australia and Canada, television carried advertising from the start, but in Britain, it was not until 1954 that the Television Act set up Independent Television (ITV), financed through advertising. ITV was immediately popular, and the income from advertising made huge profits for the TV companies. The importance of TV ratings – the number and kind of people watching – led to the growth of popular programmes like soap operas and quiz shows, which pulled in huge audiences for the ads in the natural breaks. The adverts, too, had to be entertaining to keep people watching. Some of them were like soaps themselves – Katie and her Oxo family have remained popular in different guises over the years. Others made an impact through comedy characters, jingles and catch-phrases.

LEFT In the affluent 1960s, US car advertisers linked their product to a glamorous lifestyle.

Independent Local Radio (ILR) began in 1971 and became a popular advertising medium for small local businesses. But it was not until 1990 that Independent National Radio began. Advertising has continued to grow with the development of cable and satellite television. Advertisers increasingly use sponsorship of motor racing, football and the arts to reach audiences. Direct sponsorship of programmes like the weather forecast keeps brand names in front of the viewer day after day. A new medium has been found in computer games. Advertisements for Coca-Cola and Penguin biscuits reach a teenage market in the Sega games 'Olympic Gold' and 'James Pond 2'.

ABOVE The manufacturers of Marlboro cigarettes keep their name in the public eye by sponsoring motor racing teams.

Activities

• Listen to the ads on your local independent radio station. Discuss what makes an effective radio ad. Then script and record on tape a 30-second advertisement for a local event or business.

• Write a letter to your local independent radio station asking for a copy of their advertising rate card. Compare the cost for your ad at different times and on different days of the week.

the business
of advertising

Most big companies like Quantas Airlines or Seiko sell their goods and services throughout the world. So, as part of the global marketing process, the biggest advertising agencies operate on a world-wide basis. Saatchi & Saatchi Compton, for example, works throughout Europe as well as in the USA and Australia. In the UK there are agencies at work in most large towns and cities, but the biggest agencies are based in London. Agencies become famous for particular campaigns. J Walter Thompson produced the award-winning `Beattie' ads for British Telecom, and McCann Erickson created the on-off romance for Nescafé Gold Blend. Agencies vie with each other to win the multi-million pound accounts of the big-spending names like Cadbury and Shell. The advertising agency is the link between the firms that want to advertise and the media that will carry the advertisements.

BELOW
Members of an
advertising
agency work
on plans for a
new campaign.

Not all businesses use agencies – small businesses may put together their own small ads or ask the advertisement departments of local newspapers and radio stations to design an ad for them. But, for the big national and international companies, advertising is a sophisticated part of the 'marketing mix' – the strategy that a marketing department uses to launch a new product or keep up its sales of familiar lines.

Most firms do not have specialist staff with the skills to create a large-scale advertising campaign. So they call in an advertising agency.

Once an advertising agency has been approached, the key person is the *account executive*. This representative of the agency will look after the advertiser's business, which is called an account. First, the account executive will meet the advertiser (the client) to get some background information. They will discuss the advertising budget,

ADVERTISING AGENCY

MEDIA DEPT.
Media planner
plans most effective strategy

Media buyer
buys best value media space

CLIENT COMPANY
Marketing Manager

Account Executive
liaises with client

CREATIVE DEPT.
Creative Director

Art Director
Designs layout,
images, storyboards

Copywriter
Plans words,
scripts

(Production teams)
(TV, graphics, printing)

THE MEDIA

Press

TV

Radio

Outdoor

Cinema

*(Media Sales
staff)*

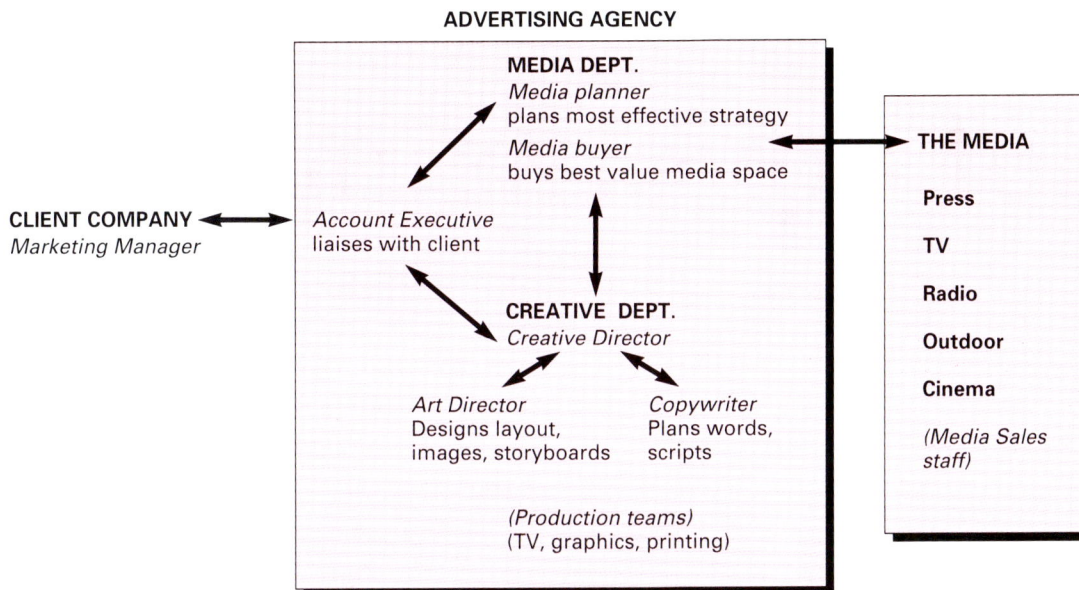

ABOVE Roles in an advertising agency.

and the product. The account executive will need to know the product's price, the market it's aimed at, and its main selling points, as well as those of the competition. The agency may carry out some market research to identify the target audience and the best way to get the message through to them.

Once they have the answers, the account executive and his or her team have a better idea of what they must do to persuade their audience. They will meet to plan the campaign. The size of the team depends on the agency – a large agency with big accounts will have many specialists looking after separate areas of the work. In smaller ones people will carry out several different

jobs. The account executive keeps in touch with the client, but also works with experts in the different aspects of advertising.

The *media planner* knows all about the different media and which will most effectively reach the target audience. Media planners have information at their fingertips about the audience profiles of all media. For example, they know that *Just Seventeen*'s readership is older than *Jackie*'s. They use classification tables (see page 24) that label people according to their occupations, and they know which media reach the better-off ABCs. They also categorize people according to age and life style, and place ads accordingly. So ads for a

Daily Telegraph full page	**£29,500**
Sunday Times full page (Section A)	**£44,000**
Radio Times full page (black and white)	
(in mid/late television programmes)	**£13,500**
Jackie full page (black and white)	**£1,904**
full page (colour)	**£2,710**
Glasgow Herald full page	**£8,215**
ITV/London 30 second weekday peak time spot	
(5.15pm - 8.00pm)	**£38,000**
Scottish Television 30 second weekday peak time spot	
(5.00pm - 10.45pm)	**£10,000**
London Cinemas (327 screens)	
30 second spot (each day, one week)	**£19,836**
BRMB Radio Birmingham	
30 second weekday spot (4.00pm - 6.00pm)	**£170**
source: Advertising Association	

karaoke challenge are placed in *Smash Hits*, while conservatories are advertised in *House & Garden*. Many other systems are used: in the USA, media planners use PRIZM, which gives different groups snappy titles – 'Young Influentials', 'Pools and Patios', and 'New Homesteaders'.

The *media buyer* knows how to negotiate with the different media to get the best deal.

ABOVE
Examples of advertising rates.

BELOW
Designers try out ideas for the artwork of an advertisement.

Media buyers often use *BRAD* (British Rate and Data), a monthly reference book which lists the rates charged by all the media, to find the biggest coverage at the most economical price. Most agencies deal mainly with 'above the line' media, that is TV, radio, the press, cinema and outdoor advertising. Some also handle 'below the line' media from direct mail and exhibitions through to beer mats and car stickers.

When the right media for the adverts have been chosen, the *creative director* will work with the *copywriters* and *art directors* to plan the ads. These people are the persuaders, who have brainstorming sessions where they think up the most original line and the most telling image. The art director designs the way the ad will look, and works with layout artists and typesetters to create the maximum impact. They work closely with the copywriters, who write slogans and catchwords. Their job is to make the words (known as copy) work to get the message across in the most effective way. Advertising teams like this have created ideas for famous advertisements – like the 'pregnant man' ('Would you be more careful if it was you that got pregnant?'), and the Levi's launderette stripper.

After much working and re-working of ideas, the team will make a final presentation of their planned campaign to the client. They will show mock-ups of poster and press adverts, or storyboards and jingles for TV commercials. They will also show the costings for their choice of media. If the ideas are accepted by the client, the team swings into action on the complex task of getting the finished adverts into production. Studios will produce finished artwork and copy, or a production team may be hired to film commercials. Media planners and buyers will make final arrangements for the advertisement to appear in the chosen media. Time is often of the essence – ads for ice-creams must be ready for the summer and those for Christmas toys by November.

There is still work for the agency to do. After the ads have appeared, the agency needs to report on how well the campaign has worked. This is always difficult to measure, but market researchers will ask people if they have noticed the ads for the product and, more importantly, if they have bought it, or would do so in future. Trade magazines of the industry, like Campaign and Marketing, often report on the success of particular campaigns.

ABOVE
The advertising team meets to discuss the results of its creative work.

We have seen how the advertising agency works for the client, but we must not forget the third partner in the process – the newspapers, magazines, TV and radio which make up the main media. These could not exist in their present form without selling advertising space. This is the job of the media sales people. They offer different rates according to the placing or timing of the space. In newspapers, for example, there are different rates for different days of the week and for different positions in the paper. In television, rates charged for ads vary according to a number of factors. The most important of these is the ratings – the numbers watching the programmes. Good ratings attract advertisers. TV companies can charge more for a prime-time slot in the middle of *Coronation Street* or *Darling Buds of May*, than, say, an old movie in the early hours of the morning. This is why the media are so concerned with the ratings tables. These confirm the size of audiences for radio and television, newspapers and magazines. The Broadcasters' Audience Research Board (BARB) covers ratings for television, while the Joint Industry Committee for National Readership Surveys (JICNARS) confirms the numbers of readers of newspapers and magazines. So advertisers can know quite precisely the numbers and type of people that an advert can expect to reach.

RIGHT Advertising agencies hire specialist video production teams to film television commercials.

BELOW Social classification table.

Grade	Occupations	Approximate % of UK population
A	Higher managerial, administrative and professional (eg Company Director, Doctor)	2.7
B	Middle managerial, administrative and professional (eg Manager, Teacher, Nurse, Engineer)	14.0
C1	Supervisory or clerical and junior managerial, administrative and professional (eg Shop Assistant, Bank Clerk)	26.3
C2	Skilled manual (eg Carpenter, Machinist)	24.9
D	Semi-skilled and unskilled manual (eg Cook, Waiter)	19.1
E	Casual labourers, state pensioners & unemployed	12.9

source: Advertising Association

Activities

• As a group, plan and carry out an advertising campaign in your school, taking the roles in an advertising agency. Choose an event, a cause or an idea you want to publicize. Then:

i) Consider your purpose, target audience and available media. Do any necessary market research and plan your media strategy.

ii) Draft your copy and artwork.

iii) Make a presentation of your campaign to the class for comment.

iv) Produce your finished advert for reproduction or display.

how
advertisements work

Advertisers want to discover the most effective techniques of persuasion. However, some people have argued that advertising cunningly persuades us to buy things that we don't really need. These critics of advertising argue that the public needs to protect itself against advertising. So a great deal of research has been carried out into how advertisements work. You will recognize the use of the following techniques if you look critically at current posters, press adverts and TV commercials.

A simple technique for fixing an idea in the memory is repetition. The brand name of a product usually appears many times in an ad so that it lodges in the mind. Key words are often repeated several times, for example words like 'fresh' or 'country' in ads for cheese, eggs, yoghurt and butter. The ads themselves are repeated over a period of time, to increase their impact. An evening's TV often gives an ad several exposures to drive the message home.

LEFT
1940s cricket star Denis Compton encourages his fans to use Brylcreem.

Another technique with a long tradition is the appeal to authority. Some adverts for toothpaste claim that dentists recommend the product. People need to have confidence in ads and the use of doctors' and nurses' recommendations can boost a product. Reference to 'scientific research' is also used to promote products. But advertisers have to be careful – manufacturers of vitamin pills that claimed to improve the intelligence of children had to abandon their claim after the research on which it was based was questioned. In some adverts, goods are endorsed by stars. The advertisers hope that their popularity will rub off on the product.

RIGHT
In this 1940s advertisement, doctors lend their authority to Camel cigarettes – unthinkable today when the danger of smoking is widely known.

TV ads, in particular, use humour to keep their audiences watching. A lively, jokey ad will appeal to the audience and hold its attention. Heineken's running joke – the beer that 'reaches the parts that other beers cannot reach' – uses this technique. Sometimes humour is linked with an ongoing storyline or with entertaining characters like the chimps in the PG Tips ad.

BELOW
Animated puppets are popular in humorous ads. These talking pigs advertise electric showers.

Many ads appeal to the reason by supplying factual information. But many more work by appealing to our basic needs and desires. Advertisers try to find out what we want and then show us how they can supply it. An advert for sun cream, for example, will stress how it will prevent sunburn and give us an attractive golden tan. But we also have deeper needs and desires, some of them unconscious, which advertisers play on. For example, copywriters often incorporate the word 'home' or 'family', both of which suggest warmth, comfort, and security – all deep-seated needs. Again, advertisers know that most people desire to be physically attractive and this is constantly used in ads for cosmetics, clothes and beauty products, especially for women. People want to 'keep up with the Joneses', and advertisers often trade on this, whether they are providing for the latest teenage craze or state-of-the-art business systems. Many people have a particular need for status and power. Car adverts present cars as status symbols and airlines stress the special treatment that is offered to the successful business executive. On the other hand, some adverts work through our fear of certain things. The early Aids ads stressed the terror of an uncontrolled disease, and a recent

MORE THAN JUST WHITE—SPOTLESS!
That sheet is spotless because Mummy boiled it in Surf. That's why she's so happy—every spot and stain came out. And what's more, Surf made a wonderful job of the coloureds too. Washday has been a complete success. Everything is spotless—because Surf is the first complete detergent.

JUST LOOK AT THE SHEET in this picture. Spotless—after one good boil in Surf. And that's where Surf has an enormous advantage over other detergents. *You can boil in Surf!* That's what makes Surf the world's first complete detergent. WITH SURF IN THE COPPER every trace of dirt rolls out. Stains vanish. Surf gives a spotless boil . . . all your white things come

out spotlessly white. See how Surf deals with babies' nappies, and you'll know. They come out of a Surf boil snowy white, yet soft enough, cuddly enough to make baby coo with delight. COLOURED THINGS love a Surf wash too. Surf brings up all their true colours and wins back their original gayness and freshness even if they're no longer new.

AND THOUSANDS OF HAPPY WOMEN who use Surf every week will tell you that Surf makes water soft as rain to your hands. Next washday, try Surf. Everything—your coloureds as well as whites—will be spotless, because Surf is the world's first complete detergent. Family size 1 11d. Handy size only 1 -.

For a Spotless Boil you need Surf

THE WORLD'S MOST COMPLETE DETERGENT

Surf

ABOVE
Washing powder ads have always played on the idea that women should prove themselves good wives and mothers.

government ad on car theft presented petty criminals as ravening hyenas.

Most advertisements employ these techniques through a variety of elements – words, images, perhaps colour, music and other sounds – and these work together to appeal to our hearts and minds. Any ad has to be constructed, or put together, by the advertising team, and so can be deconstructed, or taken apart, by those of us who want to know how it works.

Most adverts follow the formula AIDA – every ad must attract ATTENTION, arouse INTEREST, create DESIRE and make ACTION easy. Let's see how this works for the advert for Barclays Student Bank Account on page 30. The advert is squarely aimed at a small but well-defined audience – those who are going to university or college for the first time. It's an important audience for a bank to reach because most people stay with their first bank for life. How does the advert try to win over this group?

How does it attract ATTENTION?

The Ad speaks directly to students. The headline uses a witty play on words which is contrasted with the amusing picture. This is positioned slightly above centre, to give a strong focus to the ad. The fact that the 'student' is a dog with a sophisticated air gives the image an entertaining twist, intriguing the reader and encouraging him or her to read on.

How does it arouse INTEREST?

Students will associate the relaxed 'student' with themselves – it is leading the life they perhaps secretly hope to lead as a student. In this role they will reap the rewards for all their previous years of study. They can relax with sport,

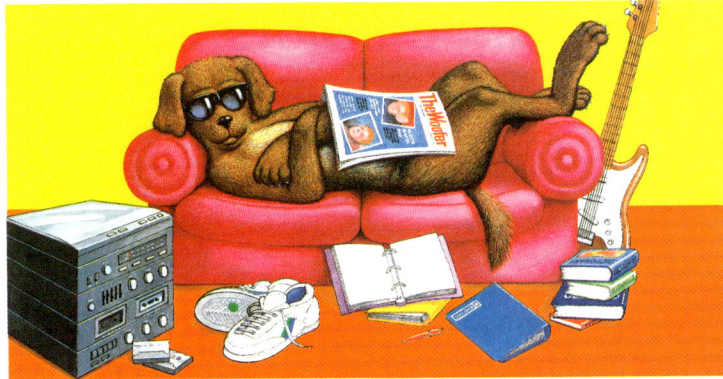

Students,
when you're working like a dog
Barclays won't hound you
for interest on your overdraft.

Interest free overdraft facilities of up to £300 available at any time during your course.

Open a Barclays Student Bank Account and you may apply for interest free overdraft facilities of up to £300, at any time during your course. There's Barclays Connect card (a 3 in 1 debit, cash dispenser and cheque guarantee card). There are no bank charges for everyday sterling transactions within the UK and you'll receive interest on credit balances.

We've also got over 6,200 cash dispensers in our network.

£10 Our Price Music voucher.

As an added bonus, we'll give you a £10 music voucher to use at Our Price Music stores.

And when you want information and help you'll find a Student Business Officer at branches near colleges.

So, go down to your nearest branch or post the coupon to Student Bank Account Service, Barclays Bank Information Centre, PO Box 63, Freepost, Coventry CV4 8BR and we'll send you details.

Or, of course, you could just get on the dog and bone.

Please send me details of the Barclays Student Bank Account.

Surname (Mr/Ms/Miss/Mrs)_____

Forename(s) in full_____

Home Address_____

_____

_____

Postcode_____ Tel. no _____

Most convenient branch (if known) _____

FOR FURTHER INFORMATION CALL THE BARCLAYS INFORMATION LINE ON 0800 400 100 FREE.

The £10 Our Price music voucher offer closes 31st May 1993 and only one voucher will be issued per new account customer once a grant cheque or parental funds are paid into the account.

Barclays student offer is available to students entering full time education in Great Britain in 1992 on a degree course or a course such as BTEC higher award or HND. You have to be 18 or over to apply for an overdraft (20 in Jersey). Subject to status. The granting of overdraft facilities and the issue of Barclays Connect card are subject to the Bank's discretion. Call in at your nearest branch for full details. Barclays Bank Plc, registered in London, England. Reg. No: 1026167, Reg. Office: 54 Lombard Street, London EC3P 3AH.

+ + + YOU'RE
BETTER OFF
TALKING TO
BARCLAYS

music and easy living, with just a few books scattered around to show they are students. Reading on, their interest may be further aroused by 'Interest FREE overdraft' in the first sentence – and as an extra come-on, the offer of up to £300! If they get to the end of the copy, the final joke may reinforce the idea that Barclays is a fun bank to be with.

How does it create DESIRE?

The wish to bank with Barclay's is partly encouraged by an appeal to the reason. There is more copy giving details of the advantages of a Barclays account – the Barclays Connect Card, no bank charges and plenty of cash dispensers. But this informative copy is linked to the desires and emotions of the student. We have seen that the image represents a desirable style of life. But the whole ad works on some of the deepest desires of young people – the desire for money, independence and freedom to behave as they wish without being nagged. The association is clear: an independent student life style goes with a Barclays Student Bank Account. The slogan at the bottom reinforces the message. And as a final incentive – the £10 Our Price Music voucher is part of the deal.

How is ACTION made easy?

The first steps are made quick and painless by offering a freephone number, which catches the eye in bold type. Alternatively, students can easily join at their local branch or by sending in the freepost coupon.

So this advert uses layout, words, images and colour to reach its target audience, appealing to both the reason and the emotions. You may have noted that the language of the small print at the bottom, explaining the limitations of the offer, is noticeably less user-friendly. The advert was timed carefully, appearing in early autumn, when students are starting college. It was targeted through national newspapers and teenage magazines.

However, we don't just read, watch or hear advertising messages without thinking about them and perhaps criticizing them. Each one of us has knowledge and experience as well as values, attitudes and beliefs that will affect what we think about the message. Some people will not respond to the Barclays ad in the way the advertiser hoped. They may not enjoy the humour; their upbringing may have convinced them that borrowing money is wrong; they may not identify with this image of student life. They will also see advertisements for other banks, and will be given advice by parents and friends. Many different things will influence their choice of bank. So no advert works in the same way with everyone. If we view adverts critically and weigh them against other sources of information, it will help us to control the way they influence us.

Activities

• Design a storyboard and script for a 30-second TV advertisement using some of the techniques discussed in Chapter 4.

• Choose a full-page magazine advertisement and deconstruct it using the AIDA formula. Write a report on your analysis.

constraints
and controls

Because of its power to persuade and influence people, it is important that advertising is monitored and controlled. Society needs to make sure that people are not taken in by misleading advertisements, or harmed by rogues and charlatans. Responsible advertisers, too, realize that the reputation of the industry depends on the truth and integrity of the claims they make in advertisements. So advertisers are controlled both by the law and by voluntary regulations laid down by the industry itself.

BELOW
This 'advertorial' for hair products is written in the style of a magazine article to gain the reader's confidence.

The Law

In Britain, there are over a hundred laws that regulate advertising. One of the most important is the Trade Descriptions Act (1968). This says that advertisers must give a fair and honest description of the goods and services they promote. It gives protection against such things as holidays that do not live up to the glowing description in the brochure, or 'roadworthy' second-hand cars which break down on the first outing. The Consumer Protection Act (1987), lays down rules especially about advertisements for sales and bargain offers that may not be what they seem. A European Commission directive limits the use of 'knocking copy' to run down the products of competitors, although this is legal in the USA. Advertisers must be careful not to break the laws on sex and race discrimination. The wording of job adverts, for example, must give everyone an equal

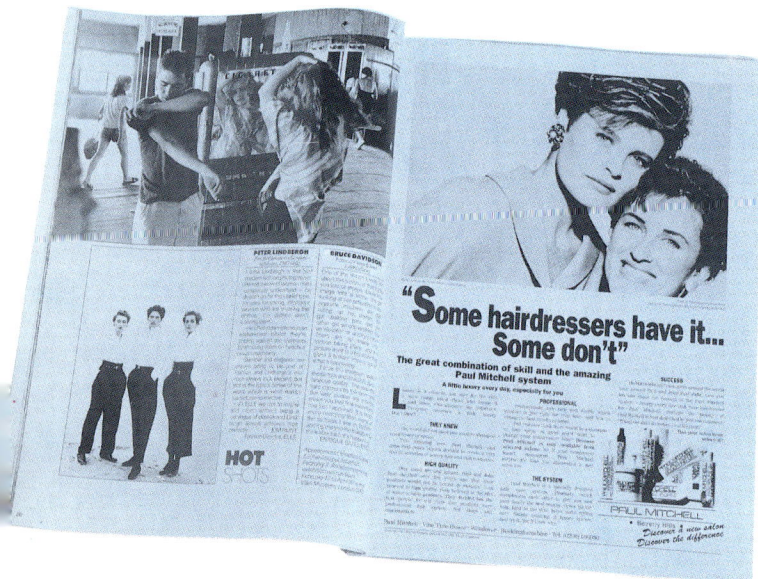

"Some hairdressers have it... Some don't"

The great combination of skill and the amazing Paul Mitchell system

The Children's Society.
Needed now more than ever.

Please send donations to: Church of England Children's Society, Freepost, London SE11 4BR. For credit card donations phone 01-735 2441.

chance to apply. Advertisers must be aware of other laws; one of the problems for advertisers working in the Single European Market is the complex network of different laws which govern advertising in the member states.

Self-regulation

In Britain, the advertising industry tries to keep its own house in order through the British Code of Advertising Practice, which all advertisers, agencies and media have agreed to uphold. It deals with all advertising except broadcasting, which is regulated separately. All adverts must be 'legal, decent, honest and truthful' and should show responsibility to consumers and society as a whole. The rules of the code make sure that advertisers do not take advantage of children, the sick, the elderly, or other groups that may be easily influenced. The code particularly spells out restrictions on ads for cigarettes and alcohol, slimming aids and medical or health cures.

ABOVE
The British Code of Advertising Practice ensures that children in charity advertisements are fairly and truthfully represented.

33

The 'watchdog' that enforces the code is the Advertising Standards Authority (ASA), which gets about 8,000 complaints from the public each year. If a complaint is upheld, the offending advertisement is withdrawn. In 1987, there were over 200 complaints about an advert for *Today* newspaper, which showed political party leaders apparently hanging from nooses. The ASA requested that it should not be used again.

BELOW
The Advertising Standards Authority encourages people to complain about offensive advertisements.

IF AN ADVERT IS WRONG, WHO PUTS IT RIGHT?

We do.

The Advertising Standards Authority ensures advertisements meet with the strict Code of Advertising Practice.

So if you question an advertiser, they have to answer to us.

To find out more about the ASA, please write to the address below.

Advertising Standards Authority, Department X, Brook House, Torrington Place, London WC1E 7HN.

ASA

This space is donated in the interests of high standards

In 1992, the Italian clothes company, Benetton, caused offence to many by its poster showing a newborn baby, complete with streaks of blood and mucus. Opinions of this image were mixed: some people found it distasteful, while others felt that it was acceptable because it was true to life. However, other Benetton posters, showing a nun kissing a priest, and a man dying of Aids, led to so many complaints that all the advertisements were banned by the ASA.

The Independent Television Commission (ITC) controls all commercial television broadcasting in the UK, including the fifteen ITV companies, Channel 4, BSkyB and cable television. Radio commercials are checked by the Radio Authority, which follows similar principles. Rules on television are particularly tough because TV is such a powerful medium and therefore particularly open to abuse.

RIGHT
The Advertising Standards Authority banned this controversial Benetton ad.

The ITC Code of Advertising Standards and Practice aims to ensure that TV ads are not misleading, do not encourage harmful behaviour, and do not cause offence. All TV advertisements are checked before they go on the air. Some products, such as cigarettes and

tobacco, are entirely banned from the advertising slots (though manufacturers can still get round the ban by sponsoring popular televised events like motor racing). Other goods are carefully controlled. No one under eighteen, for example, may take part in an ad for alcoholic drink, and ads must not suggest that drinking is essential for young people to have a good time. Advertising of fast cars must not show them breaking the speed limit.

The code particularly deals with adverts aimed at children, who may be easily swayed by tempting words and pictures.

35

Ads for children must not suggest that their friends will despise them if they do not have the latest toy or game. And children in ads must not be shown doing dangerous things like playing near deep water or talking to strangers, in case children watching copy this behaviour. There are rules concerning charities and religious groups. Charities must respect the dignity of those for whom they are making an appeal, and must not make people feel guilty if they do not wish to give money. Religious ads may only publicize events and activities. Audiences are protected from unscrupulous 'miracle workers' and 'faith healers' who falsely raise people's hopes and who have taken advantage of religious advertising in the USA.

The ITC code also lays down that adverts must be separated from programmes, although sponsorship of programmes is allowed. The Legal and General Insurance Company appropriately use their colourful umbrella to sponsor the weather forecast. The code expressly bans subliminal advertising. This is where a message is flashed on the screen so briefly that the audience is not aware of having seen it and yet may be influenced by it.

LEFT Sexist ads like this one from 1958 used to be common, but would not be acceptable in today's society.

We should not forget that audiences can exert a strong influence on advertising and can even force adverts to be withdrawn. We have seen that in Britain, complaints to the Advertising Standards Authority or the Broadcasting Standards Council can encourage the industry to enforce the codes of practice. Consumers also work through bodies such as the Consumers' Association, which has over 700,000 members. Its magazine, *Which*, investigates misleading or exaggerated claims in ads. It encourages young people to take a more critical approach to ads through its other magazine, *Check-It-Out*, aimed at 10-15 year-olds. And consumer programmes like *That's Life*, *Watchdog* and *Checkpoint* make sure that advertisers who do not tow the line are exposed.

Activities

• Write a letter to the Advertising Standards Authority asking for information about their work in monitoring advertisements. Write a factsheet for students on the work of the ASA.

• Take an example of an advertisement which has been banned by the ASA. Do you think it is legal, decent, honest and truthful? Make notes and discuss your views in a group, giving evidence to support what you say.

advertising
and society

There is a continuing debate about the effect of advertising on individuals and on society as a whole. Some see it as an essential part of the communication system of a modern society. They would argue that without the different kinds of advertisements, society would be ill-informed. Advertisements like government television commercials campaigning for such things as improved road safety do serve a useful purpose. Adverts against dangerous drugs, drinking and driving and other anti-social activities also clearly provide a public service. It is important, too, that charities like Christian Aid inform the Western world about the problems faced by developing countries. Other ads tell us what is going on in the arts, the sporting world and the local community, widening our leisure opportunities.

Supporters of advertising would argue that it is a necessary part of industry – that advertising speeds up the introduction of new inventions and advanced technology. By expanding markets it reduces prices and helps to provide more jobs for people. Without advertising, we would also have less choice of magazines or newspapers. With no income from advertising to pay for the costs of production, publishers would have to charge the public more than most people could afford. There might be less choice available on independent television or radio, since all pro-grammes are paid for from the sale of advertising space. Another argument in favour of ads is simply that people enjoy them – that the humour, colour and creativity of good ads makes them justifiable as an art form that enriches our environment. Why, then, is advertising the cause of so much critical concern?

RIGHT Advertising has an important role to play in raising money for good causes.

Dreams and Unreality

One criticism is that advertising sells not only goods, but dreams and unreality. The main danger is that advertising

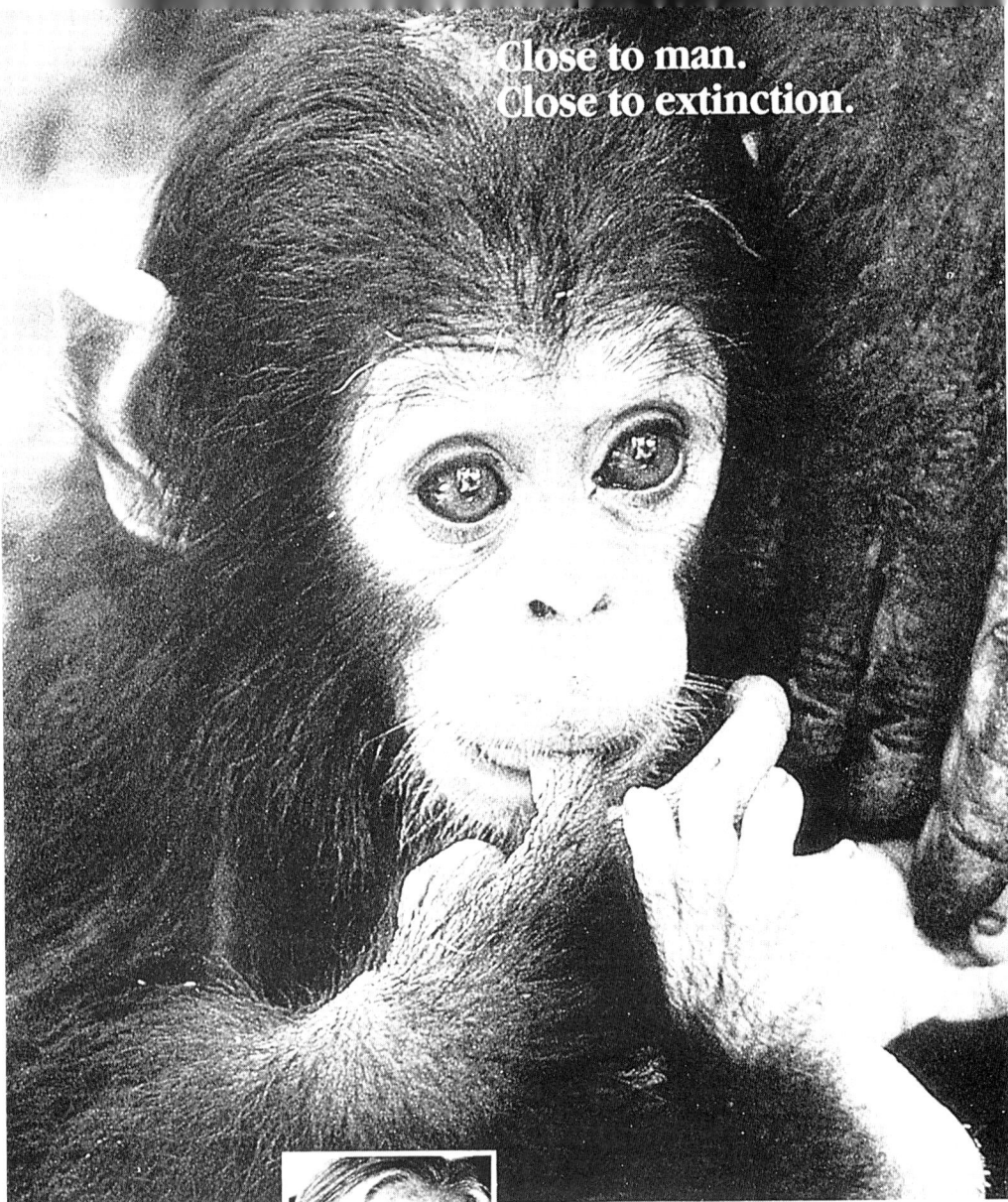

Close to man.
Close to extinction.

Do you care enough to help?

DR. JANE GOODALL

TO FIND OUT HOW TO HELP, CALL OR WRITE

The Jane Goodall Institute
For Wildlife Research, Education & Conservation

(602) 792-2075
P.O. BOX 26846
TUCSON, AZ 85726

can create desires which did not exist before, and unnecessary worries which can only be eased by responding to the advertisement. In order to sell skin cream or slimming programmes, advertisements may try to make us feel that having wrinkles or a plump figure will make us unattractive and inadequate. Some adverts encourage us to dream of a life style or appearance that we can't hope to reach. We are bound to fail in our quest and this can damage our self-confidence. The need to create new markets can be even more dangerous. In the 1980s, mothers in developing countries were persuaded by advertising that they needed to buy powdered milk for their babies instead of breast-feeding them. Because of the difficulty of sterilizing the powdered milk, this actually led to infection and deaths of babies.

BELOW
Critics claim that adverts for expensive clothes and other luxury goods make us value material things too highly.

Values of Materialism

This raises the fundamental question of who is sending advertising messages. As advertising is part of the competitive capitalist structure of the modern business world, it is the values of capitalism that dominate most advertising messages. Success means having material goods like expensive cars, jewellery and exotic holidays. The values of consumerism are reinforced by the advertising we see around us. We are constantly told that happiness and satisfaction come from buying the latest drink

RALPH LAUREN
COUNTRY

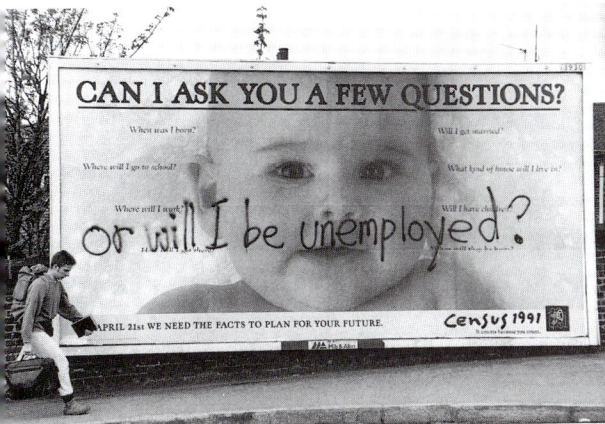

or snack bar. Only a minority of ads remind us of values such as compassion, generosity and consideration for the needs of other people.

Few groups have the money to give them access to large-scale advertising, but sometimes the values of materialism that dominate adverts are challenged by graffiti writers. A group called Active Visual Intervention (AVI) specializes in carefully altering posters to give them an alternative message. Others use spray-cans to add to or change the messages they dislike.

Representation

There is concern about the way in which certain groups are represented in advertising. Advertisers still tend to use stereotypes – fixed characterizations of groups or individuals – to get their message across quickly.

Stereotyping is a necessary part of communication, but it can be harmful. For example, Asian women are often shown in airline ads as being submissive, with their main aim to please and flatter men. Australian men are often shown to be brash and uncultured in lager adverts. If we accept these stereotypes without question, they may create prejudice against groups and prevent us from seeing people as individuals. Advertisers are now more conscious of the effect on women if they are portrayed merely as sex objects or as housewives, though the state of the weekly wash is still shown as a prime concern of women. However, there are now more ads that represent them as independent career women, in charge of their own lives. There is concern, too, about racial minority groups, who are under-represented in adverts.

LEFT
Graffiti can change or add to the meaning of an advertising message.

BELOW
In this 1930s advert, the speech and appearance of black people is ridiculed. They are also shown to be happy servants of white people. The racist attitudes of the advert would not be tolerated under today's regulations.

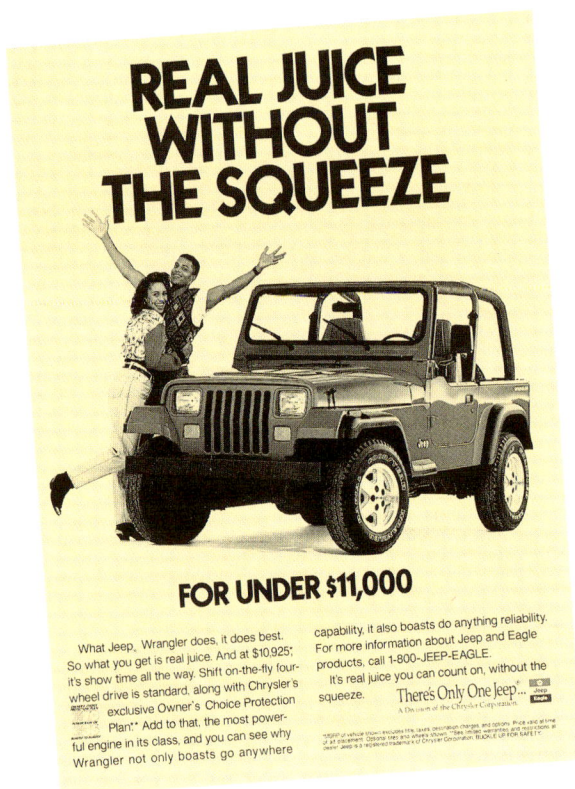

REAL JUICE WITHOUT THE SQUEEZE

FOR UNDER $11,000

What Jeep, Wrangler does, it does best. So what you get is real juice. And at $10,925, it's show time all the way. Shift-on-the-fly four-wheel drive is standard, along with Chrysler's exclusive Owner's Choice Protection Plan.* Add to that, the most power-ful engine in its class, and you can see why Wrangler not only boasts go anywhere

capability, it also boasts do anything reliability. For more information about Jeep and Eagle products, call 1-800-JEEP-EAGLE.

It's real juice you can count on, without the squeeze.

There's Only One Jeep®... Jeep Eagle

A Division of the Chrysler Corporation.

*MSRP of vehicle shown excludes title, taxes, destination charges, and options. Price valid at time of all placement. Optional hard and soft tops and others shown. Tires, wheel warranties and restrictions at dealer. Jeep is a registered trademark of Chrysler Corporation. BUCKLE UP FOR SAFETY.

Black people are very rarely the main characters in mainstream adverts, despite the fact that 5 per cent of the UK's population belongs to this group. Recently, there has been concern about the way in which people with disabilities have been represented as pas-sive objects of pity. Now, soci-eties like Mencap are changing their advertising images to show men-tally handicapped people leading active and purposeful lives. Similarly, Oxfam and other charities are concerned that people from developing countries should not be represented only as starving, helpless and dependent. Hap-pier images are showing more healthy people who are in control of their own economy.

Political Influence

Critics consider that the increased use of advertising techniques by govern-ments and political parties means that the image of politicians and parties has become more important than their ideas and ability to govern. At election times, the media are increasingly concerned with the success or failure of the parties' publicity campaigns. 'Spin doctors' are employed to advise on party political broad-casts, poster campaigns and other publicity. In the USA, Bill Clinton's successful presiden-tial campaign in 1992 owed much to the skills of the adver-tising industry, although many feel that these slick techniques are not appropriate in the serious business of a democratic election.

There is also concern about the way that parties in government use public money to promote their policies. The massive marketing campaign for the privatization of British Gas cost £40 mil-lion of taxpayers' money. Advertising is

used not only to give information, but to persuade people to approve government measures like job training schemes for young people.

Effect on the Media

Advertising is closely woven into the fabric of the rest of the media. We have seen that TV, newspapers and magazines are financially dependent on advertising. ITV is entirely funded by the sale of advertising and many newspapers get more than half their income from ads. This influences the media in many ways. The programming of independent TV and radio is heavily influenced by the need to attract large audiences for the advertisers. It is difficult for any newspaper or magazine to succeed without advertising. Newspaper editors may be under pressure not to offend the businesses which put advertisements their way, and this may affect what they have to say.

Publications sometimes run editorial features with the specific aim of attracting particular advertisers. You will also see advertising presented in the style of an editorial feature. This is known as an advertorial and should be clearly identified as advertising, though this is not always done. Sponsorship of TV programmes is another form of advertising.

The credits for The Word promote Swatch watches. Product placement – the use of branded products like soft drinks or crisps in films and videos is another way of promoting products. In these and many other ways, our television programmes, newspaper articles, computer programs and cinema screens are increasingly dominated by the messages of advertisers.

It is important that we are aware of these messages and the way they work. By understanding them, we can make an informed contribution to the continuing debate about advertising and its effect on society.

Activities

• Get a copy of your local newspaper. Measure the extent (in cm) of columns of:
i) Classified ads
ii) Display ads
ii) Advertorials/advertising features
iv) Editorial (news and features etc.)
Make a graph to show the proportions of each and comment on your findings.
• Draw up a questionnaire to find out what people think about advertising. Carry out your survey, then write a report, using graphs and tables if required.

glossary

Advertorials Advertisements presented in the same style as magazine or newspaper features.

Affluent society A society in which people are generally financially well-off and have spare money to spend. The term was used to describe some Western countries in the late 1950s and 1960s.

Audience The people receiving any communication.

Audience profile Information about a particular audience e.g. age, sex, social class, life style.

Cable television TV available to subscribers, delivered by means of underground cable.

Campaign An advertisement or series of advertisements promoting a product over a period of time.

Capitalism An economic system based on the private ownership of the means to create jobs and work; most Western countries are capitalist.

Commercial television/radio Media in which programmes are paid for by money gained from advertising.

Consumerism A way of life in which buying and spending are central activities.

Deconstruction Taking apart an advertisement or other communication in order to understand more clearly how it works.

Direct mail Advertising material sent directly to the homes of the receivers.

Dominant values Those values which are most commonly held in a society; for example, in many societies, material success is highly valued.

Graffiti Writing in public places, such as on walls or advertising posters. It is often used to change the original intention of another message.

Hoarding A large, usually wooden, structure used to carry advertisements, especially posters.

Knocking copy Advertising copy that boosts its subject by running down the competition.

Marketing Preparation for a product to be 'brought to the market' – that is, put before the consumer. There are many different marketing jobs to be done, and advertising is only one of them.

Market research Investigation into what potential buyers may want or need and into how they respond to advertising.

Mass media Any media reaching a mass audience, for example, TV, radio, the press and the cinema. Often referred to as 'the media'.

Medium Any means of communication.

Photo-opportunities Publicity events designed to provide good press or television pictures.

Press release Information sent to the news media for publication.

Pressure group A group that exerts pressure on the public or those in authority in order to change or preserve something.

Propaganda The spreading of ideas or information, usually through the mass media.

Rates The prices charged by the media for advertising space.

Ratings The numbers and type of people watching particular TV or radio programmes.

Satellite television TV using signals bounced off a satellite.

Sponsorship Paying for or towards the costs of an event such as a sports meeting, a concert or TV programme.

Status symbol Signs that indicate a person's success in material terms e.g. an expensive home or a powerful car.

Stereotype A standardized, usually over-simplified, representation of a person or group, which takes no account of individual differences.

Subliminal advertising Advertisements flashed on to a screen so briefly that the audience is not aware of having seen them, yet may be influenced by their message.

Target market The people who are likely to buy particular goods or services; the group an advertisement is aimed at.

further reading

Torin Douglas, *The Complete Guide to Advertising* (Macmillan, 1985)
Gillian Dyer, *Advertising as Communication* (Methuen, 1982)
Frank Jefkins, *Advertising* (Butterworth and Heinemann, 1992)
David Lusted, *Advertising* (Wayland, 1991)
Vance Packard, *The Hidden Persuaders* (Penguin, 1991)
Michael Pollard, *Advertising* (Penguin, 1988)

For teachers:
Manuel Alvarado, Robin Gutch and Tana Wollen, *Learning the Media* (Macmillan, 1987)
David Lusted (ed), *The Media Studies Book* (Routledge, 1991)
Len Masterman, *Teaching the Media* (Comedia, 1985)
The Marketing Pocket Book (Advertising Association, published annually), though expensive, gives useful statistics and other information used by the advertising industry.

further information and notes for teachers

Advertising can be used in a variety of ways to meet the requirements of the English National Curriculum. The examples of advertisements in their historical and social setting give opportunities for interpretation and comparison of media texts. The book provides material as a basis for three approaches to media:

i) Media languages. How do written and visual texts produce meaning?

ii) Representation. How are individuals and social groups portrayed in the advertising media?

iii) Producers and audiences. Who produces texts and why? How do audiences respond to them?

The activities are directly related to the National Curriculum, levels 6, 7 and 8, and are designed to develop critical skills and creative powers through analysis and production of media artefacts. Concepts such as purpose, audience and medium are strongly emphasized. In addition, this practical and analytical work will involve negotiation, problem-solving, group decision-making, selection and editing as well as developing communication skills.

Advertising and other books in the Media Watch series will also provide valuable material for students preparing for GCSE Media Studies and GCSE Communication.

Other sources of information include:

UK
The Advertising Association
Abford House
15 Wilton Road
London SW1V 1NJ

The Advertising Standards Authority
Brook House
Torrington Place
London WC1E 7HN

The Independent Television Commission
70 Brompton Road
London SW3 1EY

Australia
Advertising Standards Council
St Andrews House
Sydney Square
New South Wales 2000

Canada
Canadian Advertising Foundation
350 Bloor Street East
Toronto
Ontario MW4 1HA

USA
American Advertising Federation
1400 K Street
North West Suite 1000
Washington DC 2000

index numbers in **bold** refer to captions